PLACES TO EXPLORE IN AMERICA, NEW YORK 2024.

Do you want to visit New York?
Best Places To Enjoy Yourself
in New York City.

Michael J. Walk

Table of contents

Introduction

Settled in the midst of the clamoring energy of the US lies a city that typifies the quintessence of variety, culture, and development. New York City, frequently alluded to just as "NYC," remains as a reference point of chance and investigation, enamoring a huge number of guests every year with its famous milestones, lively areas, and rich embroidery of encounters.

As perhaps of the most crowded and socially different city on the planet, New York City offers an unrivaled cluster of attractions and exercises to suit each interest and tendency. From the taking off high rises of Manhattan to the varied road craft of Brooklyn, every ward flaunts its own unmistakable character and charm, welcoming explorers to set out on an excursion of disclosure and miracle.

At the core of New York City lies Manhattan, a stunning metropolitan scene portrayed by its notorious horizon and incredibly famous tourist spots. Guests can rise to the bewildering levels of the Realm State Working for all encompassing perspectives on the city, walk around the lavish desert spring of Focal Park, or submerge themselves in the dynamic energy of Times Square, where the neon lights and clamoring swarms make a charging air dissimilar to some other.

Past Manhattan, the district of Brooklyn entices with its varied blend of culture, cooking, and innovativeness. From the memorable brownstone-lined roads of Brooklyn Levels to the dynamic expressions scene of Williamsburg, there's no lack of encounters to amuse the faculties and light the creative mind. Guests can test high quality luxuries at the Brooklyn Swap meet, investigate the dynamic paintings of the Bushwick Group, or go for a comfortable walk along the picturesque waterfront of Brooklyn Scaffold Park.

Wandering further abroad, Sovereigns offers a tempting exhibit of social fortunes and unlikely treasures ready to be found. From the energetic road food scene of Flushing to the verdant magnificence of the Sovereigns Greenhouse, this different ward offers a rich embroidery of encounters that mirror the varied mosaic of its occupants and networks.

In the interim, the Bronx, frequently eclipsed by its more well known partners, flaunts its own special attractions and social milestones. Guests can investigate the celebrated history of the Bronx Zoo, drench themselves in the lively rhythms of the Amazing Concourse, or give recognition to the tradition of hip-jump culture at the General Hip Bounce Historical center.

As the doorway to America for a large number of voyagers from around the world, New York City offers a kaleidoscope of encounters that commend the rich embroidery of human undertaking and inventiveness. Whether you're attracted to the glamour and fabulousness of Broadway, the quiet excellence of Focal Park, or the clamoring energy of Chinatown, there's something for everybody to investigate and find in this energetic city.

In this aide, we will leave on an excursion through the different areas, notorious milestones, and secret fortunes of New York City, giving bits of knowledge and proposals to assist you with capitalizing on your visit to this dynamic and extraordinary objective. From the transcending high rises of Midtown to the beguiling brownstones of Brooklyn, let us dig into the essence of NYC and reveal the vast marvels that are anticipated everywhere.

Welcome to New York City: An introduction to the vibrant and diverse cityscape of New York, highlighting its rich history, cultural landmarks, and iconic attractions.

Settled on the eastern bank of the US, New York City remains as a signal of chance, variety, and vast conceivable outcomes. From its transcending high rises to its clamouring roads, the city's dynamic energy and rich embroidery of societies have made it a worldwide symbol and a magnet for visionaries and explorers from around the world.

A Short History

New York City's story starts hundreds of years prior, when Dutch pilgrims originally settled a general store called New Amsterdam in the mid seventeenth hundred years. Throughout the long term, the city developed into a flourishing center of trade, movement, and advancement, drawing in floods of novices looking for shelter, fortune, and opportunity. From the flood of European settlers in the nineteenth and mid twentieth hundreds of years to the Incomparable Relocation of African Americans from the South, New York City turned into a blend of societies, dialects, and customs.

Social Milestones

Today, New York City brags an abundance social milestones that mirror its rich and different legacy. The notable Sculpture of Freedom, an image of trust and opportunity, invites guests to the city's harbor, while Ellis Island fills in as an impactful sign of America's migrant past. In the core of Manhattan, the noteworthy neighborhoods of Chinatown, Little Italy, and Harlem offer looks into the city's multicultural texture, with lively road markets, ethnic restaurants, and social celebrations commending the practices of its occupants.

Notable Attractions

No visit to New York City would be finished without investigating its widely popular attractions. The stunning lights of Times Square, with its transcending boards and clamoring swarms, exemplify the city's throbbing energy and frantic speed. Close by, Broadway theaters grandstand the best of American theater and diversion, with blockbuster musicals, immortal works of art, and cutting edge creations charming crowds many evenings.

For workmanship darlings, the Exhibition hall Mile along Fifth Road coaxes with a gold mine of magnum opuses traversing hundreds of years and landmasses. From the Metropolitan Historical center of Workmanship's immense assortments to the cutting edge shows of the Gallery of Current Craftsmanship, New York City's social foundations offer vast open doors for motivation and edification.

Obviously, no visit to New York City would be finished without an excursion to the highest point of the Domain State Building, where all encompassing perspectives on the city's horizon stretch as may be obvious. Focal Park, a rambling desert spring in the core of Manhattan, gives a serene departure from the metropolitan buzzing about, with grand pathways, rich plant life, and famous milestones, for example, Bethesda Porch and Bow Extension welcoming guests to unwind and re-energize in the midst of nature's excellence.

As one of the world's most powerful and different urban communities, New York City keeps on moving, challenge, and spellbind all who visit its celebrated roads. From its dynamic social milestones to its notorious attractions, the city's one of a kind mix of history, inventiveness, and flexibility fills in as a demonstration of the getting through soul of human undertaking and the vast conceivable outcomes of the Pursuit of happiness. Welcome to New York City — where dreams are made, and recollections are produced in the midst of the throbbing cadence of metropolitan life.

Chapter 1: Manhattan

Settled at the core of New York City, Manhattan remains as an image of desire, variety, and social dynamism. With its famous horizon, clamoring roads, and energetic areas, Manhattan is a microcosm of the American experience — where dreams are sought after, and potential outcomes proliferate.

Topography and Format

Manhattan, lined by the Hudson Stream toward the west, the East Waterway toward the east, and encompassed by different precincts of New York City, involves a simple 22.83 square miles, yet its impact resonates across the globe. Partitioned into a few particular regions, including Midtown, Downtown, Uptown, and Harlem, every local offers an interesting embroidery of history, culture, and way of life.

Verifiable Importance

From the beginning of Dutch colonization to its development as a worldwide monetary center point, Manhattan's set of experiences is a story of versatility, advancement, and rehash. The island saw essential crossroads in American history, including the marking of the Statement of Freedom and the introduction of the cutting edge LGBTQ+ privileges development at the Stall Hotel.

Social Variety

Manhattan's social scene is all around as different as its occupants. From the elite historical centers of Exhibition hall Mile to the energetic road specialty of Lower East Side, each edge of Manhattan throbs with imagination and articulation. Its venues have momentous exhibitions, its displays feature state of the art craftsmanship, and its cafés offer a culinary excursion all over the planet.

Monetary Force to be reckoned with

As the monetary capital of the world, Manhattan is inseparable from Money Road and the worldwide economy. High rises like the Realm State Building and One World Exchange Place overwhelm the horizon, filling in as landmarks to private enterprise and desire. The city's economy flourishes with finance, innovation, media, and the travel industry, drawing in ability and speculation from each side of the globe.

Social Texture

At its center, Manhattan is a mixture of societies, dialects, and characters. From the clamoring roads of Chinatown to the luxurious stores of Fifth Road, variety is praised and embraced. Networks structure very close bonds, giving a feeling of having a place in the midst of the hurrying around of metropolitan life.

Difficulties and Open doors

However, Manhattan likewise wrestles with difficulties like pay imbalance, lodging reasonableness, and foundation strain. As the city develops, offsetting development with supportability becomes foremost. Drives to address environmental change, advance reasonable lodging, and improve public transportation highlight Manhattan's obligation to make an additional fair and versatile future.

Times Square: Explore the bustling epicenter of entertainment, shopping, and dining in the heart of Manhattan.

Settled in the core of Manhattan, Times Square stands as an energetic image of New York City's energy and charm. Eminent for its stunning lights, famous boards, and clamoring air, Times Square spellbinds guests from around the globe, offering a tangible gala of diversion, shopping, and eating encounters.

A Sparkling Desert garden of Lights

As day changes into night, Times Square wakes up with a kaleidoscope of lights that enlighten the famous bulletins and transcending high rises. Neon signs streak in an ensemble of varieties, projecting an enchanted gleam over the clamoring roads beneath. The sheer greatness of Times Square's radiance is sensational, acquiring it the epithet "The

Junction of the World" and cementing its status as perhaps of the most captured area on earth.

Amusement Event

At the core of Times Square lies an unmatched mecca of amusement. From Broadway theaters to live exhibitions and intuitive encounters, there's no lack of choices to charm and motivate guests, everything being equal. Theater lovers can get an elite creation at one of the various Broadway theaters that line the region, while music enthusiasts can delight in live exhibitions by skilled road craftsmen and entertainers.

Retail Heaven

For those with an inclination for shopping, Times Square offers an unmatched retail heaven. From lead stores of worldwide brands to idiosyncratic stores and trinket shops, there's something to fulfill each shopping impulse. Guests can peruse the most popular trend patterns, get novel New York City keepsakes, or enjoy extravagance shopping at famous retail chains — all inside the dynamic limits of Times Square.

Culinary Joys

Times Square is a gastronomic mixture, bragging a cluster feasting choices to suit each sense of taste and financial plan. From easygoing restaurants presenting exemplary New York cuts to Michelin-featured cafés offering high end food encounters, the culinary scene in Times Square is essentially as different as the actual city. Guests can enjoy world foods, enjoy connoisseur rarities, or get a light meal in a hurry — all while absorbing the lively environment of this unique locale.

The Beat of the City

Past its allure and fabulousness, Times Square fills in as the throbbing heart of New York City, mirroring the city's dynamic soul and social variety. It's where individuals from varying backgrounds combine to celebrate, investigate, and make enduring recollections. Whether it's getting a Broadway show, shopping till you drop, or essentially absorbing the electric environment, Times Square offers an extraordinary encounter that epitomizes the embodiment of NYC.

Central Park: Discover the serene oasis of Central Park, offering scenic landscapes, recreational activities, and cultural attractions.

Settled in the midst of the clamoring roads and transcending high rises of Manhattan lies a peaceful safe-haven, offering break from the metropolitan disarray — where nature flourishes and tranquility rules. Focal Park, with its extensive vegetation, winding pathways, and heap attractions, remains as a notorious image of relaxation and entertainment in the core of New York City.

An Embroidery of Nature

Focal Park's rich scenes, carefully planned via scene designers Frederick Regulation Olmsted and Calvert Vaux in the nineteenth 100 years, act as a demonstration of the agreeable concurrence of nature and metropolitan life. The recreation area's wandering pathways welcome guests to investigate its different biological systems, from verdant forests and manicured nurseries to serene lakes and flowing cascades.

Sporting Asylum

Past its regular excellence, Focal Park offers an abundance of sporting open doors for guests, everything being equal. Whether picnicking on the Incomparable Yard, paddling across the sparkling waters of the Focal Park Lake, or cycling along its picturesque pathways, there's no deficiency of exercises to appreciate. Sports lovers can participate in a round of baseball, ball, or tennis, while kids have a great time jungle gyms, merry go round rides, and intuitive instructive projects.

Social Fortunes

Focal Park isn't only a shelter for open air devotees; it is likewise a social focal point overflowing with notorious tourist spots and creative fortunes. The recreation area's glades act as stages for outside shows and dramatic exhibitions, while its various sculptures and landmarks honor authentic figures and occasions. The Focal Park Conservancy offers directed visits that enlighten the recreation area's rich history and feature its design wonders, including Bethesda Porch, Belvedere Palace, and Strawberry Fields, a recognition for the incredible John Lennon.

Local area Center

Focal Park is something other than a grand setting for relaxation and entertainment; a lively local area center encourages associations and brotherhood among occupants and guests the same. The recreation area plays host to a different cluster of occasions and social events, from social celebrations and noble cause strolls to yoga classes and bird-watching outings. Its inviting air welcomes individuals from varying backgrounds to meet up and praise the magnificence of nature and the soul of local area.

Saving a Heritage

Focal Park's getting through heritage as a darling metropolitan desert spring is a demonstration of the vision and stewardship of the individuals who have worked vigorously to safeguard and safeguard its normal excellence. The Focal Park Conservancy, established in 1980, assumes an essential part in keeping up with the recreation area's scenes, reestablishing its notable milestones, and guaranteeing that people in the future can keep on partaking in its magnificence.

Statue of Liberty and Ellis Island: Journey to these historic landmarks, symbolizing freedom, immigration, and the American dream.

Settled in the harbor of New York City, the Sculpture of Freedom and Ellis Island stand as notable images of opportunity, trust, and opportunity. For a huge number of settlers, these notable milestones filled in as entryways to another life in America, encapsulating the commitment of the Pursuit of happiness. Traveling to these locales isn't simply an actual journey yet additionally a powerful investigation of the foreigner experience and the getting through values that characterize the US.

The Sculpture of Freedom, a goliath neoclassical model talented to the US by France in 1886, fills in as a signal of freedom and edification. Planned by Frédéric Auguste Bartholdi and worked by Gustave Eiffel, Woman Freedom holds a light overhead, representing the directing light of opportunity. Her emotionless appearance and outstretched arm invite guests from around the world, helping them to remember the beliefs whereupon America was established: freedom, a vote based system, and uniformity.

As voyagers approach Freedom Island by ship, they are met with dazzling perspectives on the sculpture rising gloriously against the setting of the Manhattan horizon. Venturing onto the island, guests can investigate the gallery displays and find out about the sculpture's set of experiences, development, and imagery. They can likewise climb to the crown or platform for all encompassing perspectives on the city — a fitting vantage point from which to consider the meaning of this getting through image of opportunity.

Simply a short ship ride away lies Ellis Island, known as the "Island of Trust, Island of Tears." From 1892 to 1954, Ellis Island filled in as the essential section point for settlers showing up in the US, handling north of 12 million people looking for a superior life.

For some, this was the main look at their embraced country, a place that is known for commitment and opportunity sparkling not too far off.

Today, Ellis Island houses the Movement Gallery, where guests can follow the strides of foreigners who set out on the laborious excursion to America. Through intelligent shows, chronicled photos, and individual stories, guests gain knowledge into the difficulties and wins of the worker experience. They find out about the different rushes of migration that molded America's social embroidered artwork and added to its thriving and dynamism.

Traveling to the Sculpture of Freedom and Ellis Island isn't simply an illustration in history yet a demonstration of the persevering through soul of relocation and the quest for a superior life. An update America's solidarity lies in its variety and its capacity to welcome and embrace individuals from varying backgrounds. As guests stand in the shadow of Woman Freedom and walk the corridors of Ellis Island, they are reminded that the Pursuit of happiness isn't simply an objective but an excursion

— one set apart by versatility, constancy, and the
conviction that the sky is the limit in the place that is
known for the free.

Empire State Building: Ascend to the top of this iconic skyscraper for panoramic views of the city skyline and beyond.

The Domain State Building remains as a persevering through image of compositional ability, development, and the dauntless soul of New York City. From its beginning in the mid twentieth hundred years to its status as a worldwide symbol today, this superb high rise keeps on dazzling guests from around the world with its immortal tastefulness and stunning perspectives.

Transcending the clamoring roads of Manhattan, the Domain State Building offers unmatched vistas of the city horizon and then some. Its perception decks, situated on the 86th and 102nd floors, furnish guests with an all encompassing exhibition that stretches for a significant distance toward each path.

As guests rise to the highest point of this notable high rise, they are blessed to receive an excursion through time and history. From the Workmanship Deco hall embellished with marble and paintings to the fast lifts that whisk them heavenward, constantly is implanted with a feeling of greatness and wonderment.

After arriving at the perception decks, guests are welcomed by a stunning scene that exhibits the sheer greatness and variety of New York City. Toward the south, the transcending towers of downtown Manhattan intersperse the horizon, while toward the north, the scope of Focal Park unfurls like a verdant desert spring in the midst of the metropolitan wilderness.

However, the appeal of the Domain State Building reaches out a long ways past its structural wonders and all encompassing perspectives. It is a demonstration of human resourcefulness, versatility, and the getting through soul of yearning that characterizes the actual embodiment of New York City. From its modest starting points during the

Economic crisis of the early 20s to its getting through heritage as an encouraging sign and motivation, the Realm State Building keeps on moving stunningness and marvel in all who see it.

For guests to New York City, a visit to the Realm State Building isn't simply a touring journey — it is a journey to one of the world's most notable milestones. It is a potential for success to have on the world and wonder about the tremendousness of human accomplishment, to observe the city that never snoozes generally its brilliance, and to be helped to remember the limitless conceivable outcomes that anticipate those with the boldness to dream.

Broadway: Experience the magic of Broadway theater with world-class performances and blockbuster productions.

Broadway — the simple notice of this notorious road lights a feeling of miracle and energy in the hearts of theater devotees all over the planet. Inseparable from greatness, inventiveness, and exhibition, Broadway addresses the apex of live dramatic diversion. From immortal works of art to state of the art creations, the sorcery of Broadway rises above limits, dazzling crowds of any age and foundations.

At the core of Broadway's appeal lies its unrivaled obligation to imaginative greatness. Every year, the world's most capable entertainers, chiefs, choreographers, and planners meet on this renowned stage to rejuvenate stories in manners that are both entrancing and remarkable. Whether it's the stunning movement of a melodic, the crude feeling of an emotional play, or the inventive narrating of an exploratory creation, Broadway offers something for everybody, guaranteeing that each theatergoer gets themselves enchanted by the enchanted unfurling before their eyes.

One of the signs of Broadway is its capacity to ship crowds to universes both recognizable and fantastical. Using elaborate sets, staggering ensembles, and cutting edge innovation, Broadway creations make vivid encounters that rise above the limits of existence. Whether it's venturing into the excitement and charm of 1920s New York City with "Chicago" or leaving on an excursion to the mysterious place that is known for Oz with "Evil," Broadway permits crowds to get away from the real world and drench themselves in the captivating universes of the creative mind.

Notwithstanding its imaginative greatness, Broadway likewise fills in as a social standard, mirroring the different embroidery of the human experience. From interesting shows that tackle squeezing social issues to happy musicals that commend the human soul, Broadway creations investigate a large number of subjects and feelings, reverberating with crowds on a profoundly private level. Through the force of narrating, Broadway can motivate, teach, and elevate, encouraging compassion and figuring out in an undeniably partitioned world.

Past its imaginative and social importance, Broadway additionally holds monetary significance, driving the travel industry and creating billions of dollars in income every year. For guests to New York City, going to a Broadway show is frequently at the highest point of their schedule, giving an essential and quintessentially New York experience. From the famous marquees of Times Square to the notable performance centers of the Theater Locale, Broadway fills in as a signal of imagination and development, drawing guests from each side of the globe to observe the sorcery of live venue firsthand.

Chapter 2: Brooklyn

Settled inside the core of New York City, Brooklyn remains as a reference point of social extravagance, variety, and innovativeness. With its diverse areas, memorable milestones, and flourishing expressions scene, Brooklyn enthralls guests and inhabitants the same, offering a multi-layered embroidery of encounters ready to be investigated.

At the center of Brooklyn's charm lies its different populace, a mosaic of societies and characters that mix the precinct with essentialness and energy. From the clamoring roads of Williamsburg to the tree-lined roads of Park Slant, every local flaunts its own unmistakable person and appeal, molded by the networks that call it home. Brooklyn's social scene is a demonstration of the soul of inclusivity and acknowledgment, where people from varying backgrounds meet up to commend their disparities and offer in the lavishness of their legacy.

Past its dynamic areas, Brooklyn is saturated with history, with an abundance of notable milestones that mirror its celebrated past. From the superb region of Prospect Park to the notable Brooklyn Extension, these engineering wonders act as tokens of Brooklyn's getting through heritage and its significant job in forming the scene of New York City. Guests can follow the precinct's development through its notable areas, historical centers, and social establishments, acquiring knowledge into the assorted embroidered artwork of encounters that have formed its personality throughout the long term.

However, maybe what really separates Brooklyn is its unmatched innovativeness and creative imperativeness. From the spray painting enhanced roads of Bushwick to the incredibly famous exhibitions of DUMBO, Brooklyn fills in as a favorable place for development and articulation, sustaining the gifts of specialists, performers, and creatives from around the globe. Whether investigating the lively road workmanship scene or going to a presentation at the Brooklyn Foundation of Music, guests are drenched in a unique social scene that blossoms with trial and error and coordinated effort.

Brooklyn Bridge

Standing gloriously over the East Stream, the Brooklyn Scaffold is something other than a pathway interfacing two wards of New York City; it's a design magnum opus, an insignia of inventiveness, and a social symbol that epitomizes the soul of progress and development.

Planned by John Augustus Roebling and finished in 1883, the Brooklyn Extension was an accomplishment of designing ability relatively radical. Its exquisite suspension configuration, portrayed by transcending stone pinnacles and effortless steel links, altered span development and set new principles for sturdiness and strength. The extension traverses 1,595 feet, making it the world's longest engineered overpass at the hour of its finishing.

Past its specialized accomplishments, the Brooklyn Extension holds a unique spot in the hearts of New Yorkers and guests the same. It fills in as an essential conduit, working with the development of individuals and merchandise between the clamoring wards of Manhattan and Brooklyn. Its passerby walkway offers dazzling perspectives on the city horizon, welcoming local people and sightseers to walk around and submerge themselves in the metropolitan embroidered artwork beneath.

Besides, the Brooklyn Extension has been a wellspring of motivation for craftsmen, essayists, and movie producers for more than 100 years. Its immortal magnificence and representative importance have been caught in incalculable works of art, sonnets, and motion pictures, solidifying its status as a persevering through social symbol.

All through its celebrated history, the Brooklyn Extension has borne observer to wins and misfortunes, from stupendous festivals of finishing to grave remembrances of those died during its development. However, through everything, the scaffold has stayed an image of flexibility and solidarity, spanning actual partitions as well as the holes among at various times, custom and progress.

Today, the Brooklyn Extension keeps on spellbinding minds and motivate appreciation as one of the world's most conspicuous tourist spots. It remains a demonstration of human resourcefulness and the force of coordinated effort, helping us to remember the unlimited potential outcomes that emerge when we hope against hope and aim high.

Brooklyn Botanic

Settled inside the core of New York City, the Brooklyn Botanic Nursery remains as a desert spring of regular magnificence in the midst of the clamoring metropolitan scene. With its different assortment of plants, charming nurseries, and vivid instructive projects, the nursery offers guests a quiet retreat and a brief look into the miracles of the normal world.

Established in 1910, the Brooklyn Botanic Nursery traverses 52 sections of land and is home to more than 14,000 sorts of plants. Its different scenes, going from manicured yards to rich forests, give a territory to a wide cluster of vegetation, making it a sanctuary for both nature devotees and relaxed guests the same.

One of the nursery's most notorious elements is the Japanese Slope and-Lake Nursery, a serene desert spring propelled by customary Japanese scene plan. Here, guests can wander along winding pathways, cross angled spans, and appreciate the excellence of koi-filled lakes and flowing cascades. Cherry blooms, azaleas, and Japanese maples make an embroidery of variety that changes with the seasons, offering a blowout for the faculties all year.

Notwithstanding its Japanese nursery, the Brooklyn Botanic Nursery flaunts a few other themed gardens, each displaying a special assortment of plants and green procedures. From the fragrant blossoms of the Rose Nursery to the outlandish verdure of the Tropical Structure, there is something to amuse and motivate guests, everything being equal.

Past its dazzling scenes, the Brooklyn Botanic Nursery is focused on training and preservation. The nursery offers various instructive projects and studios intended to cultivate an appreciation for nature and advance ecological stewardship. From involved cultivating classes to directed visits drove by educated botanists, guests have the potential chance to develop how they might interpret plant science and natural frameworks.

As of late, the Brooklyn Botanic Nursery has extended its endeavors to advance maintainability and biodiversity. Drives, for example, the Local Verdure Nursery and the Spice Nursery feature the significance of local plants and their part in supporting neighborhood biological systems. Also, the nursery takes part in exploration and preservation endeavours pointed toward protecting imperilled species and natural surroundings.

Brooklyn Museum

Settled in the core of New York City's lively district of Brooklyn, the Brooklyn Gallery remains as a demonstration of the extravagance and variety of human imagination. Established in 1895, this social foundation has developed into one of the biggest and most regarded workmanship galleries in the US, flaunting a huge and varied assortment that traverses hundreds of years and landmasses.

At the core of the Brooklyn Historical center's main goal is a promise to commending the different voices and stories that shape our reality. From old civilizations to contemporary specialists, the gallery's assortment mirrors an embroidery of societies, points of view, and creative articulations. Guests are welcome to leave on an excursion through existence, experiencing magnum opuses that move, incite, and enlighten the human experience.

One of the characterizing highlights of the Brooklyn Historical center is its devotion to openness and inclusivity. Through imaginative programming, presentations, and local area outreach drives, the gallery looks to connect with crowds of any age, foundations, and interests. Whether through directed visits, instructive studios, or intuitive establishments, guests are urged to partake in the investigation and translation of craftsmanship effectively.

The historical center's super durable assortment is a gold mine of creative miracles, including a large number of mediums, styles, and classes. From old Egyptian relics to contemporary photography, from old style European compositions to African covers and materials, the Brooklyn Historical center offers an all encompassing perspective on human innovativeness across reality. Features incorporate famous works by eminent specialists like Frida Kahlo, Georgia O'Keeffe, and Andy Warhol, as well as less popular diamonds ready to be found.

Notwithstanding its super durable assortment, the Brooklyn Historical center is eminent for its dynamic timetable of impermanent shows and unique establishments. These pivoting shows offer new viewpoints on natural subjects and acquaint guests with new craftsmen, developments, and thoughts. From notable reviews to intriguing social critique, every presentation adds profundity and aspect to the gallery's always advancing story.

Past its job as a social foundation, the Brooklyn Exhibition hall fills in as a center point for local area commitment and discourse. Through associations with nearby associations, schools, and social foundations, the exhibition hall encourages associations and joint efforts that improve the texture of Brooklyn's assorted areas. By giving a stage to voices frequently minimized or ignored, the historical center heroes the upsides of consideration, value, and civil rights.

Prospect Park

Settled in the core of Brooklyn, New York, Prospect Park remains as a verdant desert garden in the midst of the clamoring metropolitan scene. Crossing more than 500 sections of land, this superb park offers guests a shelter of regular magnificence, sporting open doors, and social lavishness. From its rich glades and quiet streams to its notorious milestones and energetic local area, Prospect Park enamors the creative mind and motivates wonder.

At the core of Prospect Park lies an agreeable mix of regular scenes carefully planned by Frederick Regulation Olmsted and Calvert Vaux, the visionary modelers behind Focal Park. Here, guests are welcome to meander along winding ways concealed by transcending trees, investigate stowed away dales enhanced with wildflowers, and find the quietness of beautiful lakes and lakes. Whether picnicking on the Incomparable Yard, birdwatching in the Gorge, or cycling along the beautiful circle, there's a peaceful departure anticipating each lover of the outside.

Past its regular quality, Prospect Park brags an abundance social attractions that praise the variety and inventiveness of Brooklyn's energetic local area. The Possibility Park Zoo offers an enamoring look into the marvels of the collective of animals, while the Brooklyn Botanic Nursery exhibits a stunning cluster of greenery from around the world. The recreation area's famous tourist spots, including the Boat shelter, Audubon Center, and LeFrak Center at Lakeside, act as dynamic centers of movement, facilitating occasions, exhibitions, and instructive projects that enhance the existences of guests youthful and old.

Prospect Park isn't just a safe-haven for nature darlings and social devotees yet in addition a loved assembling place for the different networks that call Brooklyn home. From family-accommodating celebrations and shows to local area picnics and yoga classes, the recreation area's vivacious schedule of occasions encourages a feeling of brotherhood and having a place. Whether relaxing on the lush glades of Long Knoll, joining a round of pickup b-ball, or relishing a feast at the Outing House, guests are greeted wholeheartedly and embraced by the soul of solidarity and consideration that characterizes Brooklyn.

Coney Island

Settled along the southern shores of Brooklyn, New York, Coney Island remains as a guide of sentimentality, diversion, and social importance. Saturated with history and overflowing with attractions, this notable objective has caught the hearts and minds of guests for more than 100 years.

Authentic Foundation

Coney Island's story is one of development, from a peaceful ocean side retreat in the mid nineteenth 100 years to a clamoring entertainment mecca by the last part of the 1800s. Its change was filled by the consummation of the Brooklyn Scaffold in 1883, which made it effectively open to New Yorkers looking for rest from the city's buzzing about.

Famous Attractions

Fundamental to Coney Island's charm are its incredible attractions. The notable Twister thrill ride, worked in 1927, keeps on exciting riders with its stomach-stirring drops and fastener turns. Neighboring the Twister stands the Marvel Wheel, a transcending Ferris wheel offering clearing perspectives on the shore and horizon.

No visit to Coney Island would be finished without a walk around the famous footpath. Extending for almost three miles, the promenade is a lively embroidery of sights, sounds, and flavors. From exemplary arcade games and gift shops to restaurants presenting wieners and cotton sweets, a tangible pleasure typifies the soul of mid year fun.

Social Importance

Past its attractions, Coney Island holds a unique spot in American culture. It has been deified in writing, film, and music, filling in as a scenery for accounts of happiness, flexibility, and the quest for the Pursuit of happiness. Specialists and essayists have drawn motivation from its varied blend of characters, while producers have caught its ageless appeal on the cinema.

Local area and Versatility

Regardless of confronting difficulties throughout the long term, including monetary slumps and cataclysmic events, Coney Island has stayed a tough and lively local area. Nearby occupants, entrepreneurs, and urban pioneers have worked energetically to save its legacy and guarantee its proceeded with imperativeness. Today, Coney Island fills in as a demonstration of the force of local area and getting through the allure of shared encounters.

Chapter 3: Queens

Settled inside the energetic embroidery of New York City, Sovereigns remains as a different and dynamic district prestigious for its rich social legacy, mixed areas, and unmatched culinary scene. From its clamoring metropolitan focuses to its peaceful waterfronts, Sovereigns encapsulates the soul of inclusivity and development, drawing in guests and occupants the same with its extraordinary mix of custom and advancement.

Verifiable Foundation:

Initially occupied by Local American clans, Sovereigns has developed over hundreds of years into a blend of societies and networks. Its name, a recognition for Sovereign Catherine of Braganza, spouse of Lord Charles II of Britain, mirrors its pilgrim starting points. Over now is the right time, Sovereigns has been formed by floods of migration, from European pilgrims in the seventeenth hundred years to the convergence of assorted populaces in the twentieth and 21st hundreds of years, adding to its rich mosaic of societies.

Social Variety:

Sovereigns is commended for its social variety, with more than 190 dialects spoken and inhabitants hailing from each edge of the globe. From the clamoring roads of Flushing, known for its lively Asian people group and delightful cooking, to the creative territory of Astoria, home to a flourishing Greek populace and varied nightlife, every local offers a novel look into the embroidery of Sovereigns' multicultural texture. Celebrations, marches, and far-reaching developments further feature the precinct's rich legacy, encouraging a feeling of solidarity and pride among its occupants.

Tourist spots and Attractions:

Sovereigns brags a cluster notorious milestones and attractions that draw guests from all over. The Unisphere, an image of the 1964 World's Fair, remains as a demonstration of Sovereigns' job on the worldwide stage. Flushing Glades Crown Park, the precinct's biggest green space, offers a retreat from the buzzing about of city life, with its extensive yards, grand lakes, and famous designs. From the lively road craft of Long Island City to the notable destinations of Jamaica, Sovereigns features a different exhibit of compositional, social, and regular marvels ready to be investigated.

Culinary Pleasures:

Sovereigns is a heaven for food darlings, offering a culinary scene as different as its populace. From valid ethnic restaurants to popular bistros and connoisseur eating foundations, the precinct tempts the taste buds with an unending cluster of flavors and cooking styles. Whether relishing a steaming bowl of pho in Elmhurst, enjoying exquisite empanadas in Jackson Levels, or examining high-quality treats in Woodland Slopes, Sovereigns guarantees a gastronomic experience like no other.

Flushing Meadows-Corona Park

Settled in the core of Sovereigns, New York, Flushing Glades Crown Park remains as a demonstration of the city's rich history, various culture, and getting through soul of development. Traversing north of 1,200 sections of land, this rambling metropolitan desert spring offers guests a bunch of attractions, from famous milestones to serene green spaces, making it a must-visit objective for local people and travelers the same.

Verifiable Importance:

Initially considered as the site for the 1939-1940 and 1964-1965 World's Fairs, Flushing Glades Crown Park plays had a critical impact in molding the social scene of New York City. The recreation area's notorious Unisphere, an image of worldwide solidarity and progress, stays a transcending demonstration of the soul of global participation that characterized the World's Fair time.

Notable Milestones:

One of the recreation area's most unmistakable elements is the Unisphere, a treated steel globe standing 140 feet tall and weighing 700,000 pounds. Encompassing the Unisphere, guests can investigate the remainders of the World's Fair grounds, including the New York State Structure with its particular "Tent of Tomorrow" and the Sovereigns Exhibition hall, which houses a tremendous assortment of workmanship and memorabilia from the fairs.

Social Attractions:

Notwithstanding its verifiable importance, Flushing Glades Crown Park is home to a different cluster of social attractions. The Sovereigns Greenhouse welcomes guests to drench themselves in the excellence of nature, with themed gardens, instructive projects, and unique occasions consistently. Close by, the Sovereigns Gallery offers a rich social encounter, with pivoting shows, intelligent establishments, and local area outreach drives that praise the district's dynamic legacy.

Sporting Open doors:

For those looking for outside experience, Flushing Glades Crown Park offers sufficient chances for diversion and unwinding. The recreation area flaunts broad green spaces, jungle gyms, and sports offices, making it an ideal objective for picnics, sports associations, and family excursions. Guests can likewise appreciate paddle drifting on Glade Lake, go for a comfortable walk along the recreation area's beautiful paths, or just luxuriate in the serenity of its regular environmental elements.

Local area Commitment:

Past its job as a vacation spot, Flushing Knolls Crown Park fills in as a lively center of local area life. From social celebrations and shows to youth programs and natural drives, the recreation area encourages a feeling of having a place and community pride among occupants of any age and foundations. Its different cluster of conveniences and exercises mirrors the rich embroidery of Sovereigns' multicultural personality, making it the dearest gathering place for the ages of New Yorkers.

Queens Botanical Garden

Settled in the core of Sovereigns, New York, the Sovereigns Greenhouse stands as a peaceful desert garden in the midst of the clamoring cityscape. Spreading over 39 sections of land, this verdant asylum entices guests to submerge themselves in the excellence of nature while finding a variety of agricultural marvels.

Authentic Beginnings and Mission:
Laid out in 1946, the Sovereigns Professional flowerbed has developed into a loved social foundation committed to advancing natural stewardship and maintainability. Its main goal is to encourage an appreciation for plants, gardens, and the regular world through instruction, effort, and protection endeavors.

Herbal Variety:

One of the characterizing highlights of the Sovereigns Professional flowerbed is its assorted assortment of greenery, cautiously organized to exhibit the rich embroidered artwork of vegetation from around the globe. Guests can meander through themed gardens, each offering an extraordinary organic encounter. From the dynamic shades of the Rose Nursery to the serene excellence of the Forest Nursery, there is something to amuse each nature lover.

Instructive Projects and Effort:

Integral to the Sovereigns Greenhouse's main goal is its obligation to training and local area commitment. The nursery offers a great many instructive projects and studios for guests of any age, covering subjects like planting, supportability, and protection. Through these drives, the nursery looks to engage people to become stewards of the climate and promoters for biodiversity.

Feasible Practices:

With regards to its main goal of natural stewardship, the Sovereigns Professional flowerbed focuses on manageability in its tasks and practices. From treating the soil and water gathering to natural planting strategies, the nursery fills in as a model for manageable metropolitan cultivation. Guests are welcome to find out about these drives and find how they can integrate eco-accommodating practices into their own lives.

Comprehensive developments and Local area Commitment:

Past its herbal contributions, the Sovereigns Professional flowerbed fills in as an energetic social center point, facilitating different occasions and shows over time. From occasional celebrations celebrating social practices to craftsmanship establishments propelled naturally, the nursery encourages a feeling of local area and association among guests from different foundations.

Chapter 4:The Bronx

Settled inside the core of New York City, The Bronx remains as a demonstration of the dynamic embroidery of variety, culture, and versatility that characterizes the pith of metropolitan America. From its modest starting points as farmland to its development into a clamoring ward overflowing with life, The Bronx has made a permanent imprint on the texture of American history and culture.

The tale of The Bronx starts hundreds of years prior, when it was occupied by the Lenape Local American clan. With the appearance of European pioneers in the seventeenth 100 years, the scene changed into rambling farmland, specked with domains and towns. In any case, it was the quick industrialization of the late nineteenth and mid twentieth hundreds of years that really formed The Bronx into the powerful metropolitan scene it is today.

One of the characterizing highlights of The Bronx is its social variety. From the dynamic Latinx people group of the South Bronx to the flourishing African American neighborhoods of Morrisania and Wakefield, the ward is a mixture of dialects, cooking styles, and customs. This rich embroidery of variety has led to a dynamic social scene, with incredibly famous organizations, for example, the Bronx Gallery of Human expression and the Bronx Zoo filling in as mainstays of creative and instructive greatness.

Regardless of confronting difficulties like destitution, wrongdoing, and metropolitan rot in the last 50% of the twentieth 100 years, The Bronx has shown a noteworthy soul of flexibility. Local area drove drives, grassroots activism, and interest in financial advancement have revived areas and changed once-dismissed spaces into dynamic center points of action.

One can't examine The Bronx without referencing its commitments to music, craftsmanship, and mainstream society. From the introduction of hip-bounce in the South Bronx to the scholarly tradition of creators like Edgar Allan Poe, The Bronx has been a favorable place for imagination and development. Its roads have reverberated with the hints of jazz, salsa, and underground rock, while its walls have been embellished with lively paintings and spray painting craftsmanship.

Lately, The Bronx has encountered a renaissance, with restored revenue and venture powering its proceeded with development and improvement. From the renewal of the waterfront along the Harlem Stream to the development of new private and business improvements, the precinct is encountering a resurgence that vows to shape its future for a long time into the future.

Chapter 5: Staten Island

Picture of Staten Island

Settled at the core of New York Harbor, Staten Island remains as an unexpected, yet invaluable treasure inside the clamoring city of New York City. Frequently eclipsed by its more well known partners, Manhattan, Brooklyn, and Sovereigns, Staten Island brags a one of a kind mix regular excellence, rich history, and dynamic networks, making it an objective deserving of investigation.

Topography and Scene:

Staten Island's geology is characterized by its assorted scene, going from beautiful waterfronts to moving slopes and lavish plant life. The island is encircled by the quiet waters of the harbor, offering staggering perspectives on the Manhattan horizon and the Sculpture of Freedom. Inland, rambling parks and nature holds give safe-haven to untamed life and potential open doors for outside entertainment, making it a sanctuary for nature fans.

History and Legacy:

With a set of experiences going back hundreds of years, Staten Island is saturated with rich social legacy. Initially possessed by Local American clans, the island later turned into an essential station for Dutch and English pilgrims during the frontier time. Today, leftovers of this pioneer past should be visible in the notable tourist spots and enchanting areas that dab the island. From the notorious Staten Island Ship to the memorable destinations of Richmond Town, the island's set of experiences wakes up every step of the way.

Social Variety:

Staten Island's social scene is all around as different as its topography. Home to a blend of nationalities and networks, the island flaunts a lively social scene that commends its varied legacy. From dynamic celebrations and widespread developments to elite feasting and shopping, Staten Island offers a sample of worldwide culture directly in the core of New York City.

Attractions and Milestones:

Notwithstanding its generally little size, Staten Island is overflowing with attractions and milestones ready to be found. The Staten Island Zoo offers a brief look into the animals of the world collectively, while the Staten Island Gallery features workmanship, science, and history shows. For outside fans, the Greenbelt Conservancy gives miles of climbing trails and picturesque ignores, while the Staten Island Greenhouse offers a serene break in the midst of lavish gardens and blossoming blossoms.

Local area and Way of life:

What genuinely separates Staten Island is its feeling of local area and easygoing way of life. Distant from the hurrying around of Manhattan, the island offers a more slow speed of life, where neighbors welcome each other with a well disposed grin and occupants invest wholeheartedly in their affectionate networks. Whether going to a neighborhood road fair, giving a shout out to the Staten Island Yankees at the ballpark, or basically partaking in a comfortable walk around the waterfront, life on Staten Island is characterized by its feeling of local area and association.

Made in the USA
Las Vegas, NV
03 June 2024

90701227R00039